Faces

OF HEARST CASTLE

Faces

OF HEARST CASTLE

JANA SEELY & KERI COLLINS

HEARST CASTLE
PRESS

Faces of Hearst Castle by Jana Seely and Keri Collins

Photography and book design by Gary Ashcavai

First Edition

Publisher's Cataloging-In-Publication Data
(Prepared by The Donohue Group, Inc.)

Seely, Jana.
  Faces of Hearst Castle / Jana Seely & Keri Collins ; photography and book design by Gary Ashcavai. -- 1st ed.

   p. : col. ill. ; cm.

  Includes bibliographical references and index.
  ISBN-13: 978-0-9792156-3-6
  ISBN-10: 0-9792156-3-3

1. Face in art--Catalogs. 2. Hearst Castle (Calif.) 3. Hearst, William Randolph, 1863–1951--Art collections. I. Collins, Keri. II. Ashcavai, Gary. III. Title.

N7573.3.S44 2007
704.942   2006940986

Hearst Castle Press operates as a separate division of Friends of Hearst Castle, a 501(c)(3) nonprofit cooperating association.

Photo, Fig. 5 courtesy of Hearst Castle Archives

CONTENTS

Fig. 1 (above): "Madonna and Sleeping Child," Giovanni Battista Salvi, known as Sassoferrato (1609-1685), Italian, oil on canvas. H: 29"; W: 24".

Fig. 2 (opposite): Casa Grande

INTRODUCTION

From the moment of birth, humans rely on facial recognition. The bond between caretaker and child is forged so early in life it appears innate, as an infant can almost instantaneously distinguish between the mother's face and all others. While human faces are made up of the same components and are thus very similar in form, each face is rendered unique by the subtle variations that define an individual and facilitate identification. Creatures of habit, humans are drawn to the familiar, and nothing is more familiar than a face. As highly social beings, our art reflects our preference for what we know.

2.

Publisher and movie producer William Randolph Hearst surrounded himself with art from all over the world, and his collection manifests a global fascination with myriad faces, encompassing the divine and the earthly *(Fig. 1)*. Hearst's estate, now an historic house museum accessible to the public, showcases art indoors and out, on walls and windows, floors and faucets, ceilings and stairs. Characters from history, mythology, religion, nature, and imagination inhabit the fine and decorative arts on display. Faces are everywhere.

An art collector from an early age, William Randolph Hearst grew up as the privileged son of miner-politician George Hearst and philanthropist Phoebe Apperson Hearst. Encouraged by his mother's interest in cultural pursuits, he explored Continental Europe and the British Isles during an eighteen-month trip that began when he was ten years old. This experience contributed to a lifelong love of travel, an interest in architecture, and a passion for art which culminated in the construction of La Cuesta Encantada (The Enchanted Hill) in San Simeon, California *(Fig. 2)*.

Called "the Ranch" by Hearst but today more commonly known as Hearst Castle, the hilltop estate was designed by architect Julia Morgan in collaboration with Hearst. Overlooking the Pacific Ocean, the Mediterranean Revival-style complex of structures—a main house, known as Casa Grande, three guesthouses, and two swimming pools—connected by gardens and tiled pathways, is the result of a nearly thirty-year building project (1919–1947). Plans for the estate waxed and waned according to Hearst's finances and his caprices.

What never faltered was the incorporation of art into all aspects of construction. When designing the structures and interiors, Julia Morgan capitalized on the

3.

wealth of objects Hearst acquired. She borrowed designs from classical examples *(Fig. 3)* and had them replicated in modern materials to be used in multiples where appropriate. When a suitable antique could not be procured, Hearst and Morgan pored over books for design ideas and consulted dealers who would sometimes provide photos, plans, or sketches for inspiration *(Fig. 4)*. Another strategy was adapting antique objects to fulfill new purposes *(Fig. 5)*.

4.

Hearst Castle's many treasures have been maintained by California State Parks since the donation of the property in 1957. Because the San Simeon estate was only part of William Randolph Hearst's extensive holdings, the records, inextricably bound with those of privately held business interests, did not accompany the gift. Consequently, limited definitive documentation is available. The breadth of the collection's scope, coupled with incomplete information about specific items, has thus far

5.

made publication of an exhaustive catalogue impractical. *Faces of Hearst Castle* serves to highlight select artifacts, many of which have benefited from recent scholarship. The objects, representing a microcosm of the whole, were photographed in place to preserve the essence of their context as part of the household furnishings of a unique country estate.

Each of the following faces tells a small part of the story of William Randolph Hearst's Enchanted Hill.

Fig. 3 (opposite above): Double Bust, Greco-Roman, 2nd century B.C., marble. H: 10 ½"; W: 7 ½"; D: 7 ¾". Hearst-era craftsmen replicated this design and adapted it to create cast stone lamp standards.

Fig. 4 (opposite below): Left: Ceiling Panel, Van der Loo, 20th century, cast plaster, gilt, polychrome. Right: Watercolor sketch, Arthur and Mildred Stapley Byne, 1921, H: 10 ½"; W: 14 ½". The watercolor sketch of the original ceiling panel from Casa de los Tiros (House of the Heroes) in Granada, Spain, was used in recreating a ceiling installed in Casa del Mar.

Fig. 5 (above): Sarcophagus, Roman, 3rd century, marble. H: 28 ½"; W: 89 ½"; D: 31". Originally a stone tomb, this sarcophagus featuring the Nine Muses flanking a portrait of the deceased as Apollo, is now a garden ornament.

"BONAPARTE BEFORE THE SPHINX"

(ALSO KNOWN AS "OEDIPUS"), JEAN-LÉON GÉRÔME
(1824–1904), FRENCH, OIL ON CANVAS, 1867–68.
H: 24 ¼"; W: 40 ½"

Seen in profile with his cavalry reduced to shadows behind
him, the French general contemplates the ancient enigma of
the Sphinx's visage. The depiction of scenes like this evolved
in response to foundational work created by the cadre of
artists and antiquarians who accompanied Napoleon on
his unsuccessful Egyptian military campaign of 1798. The
work of these artists eventually helped catalyze a movement
known as "Orientalism," since at that time, the Orient
was perceived to include North Africa and the Near East.
Gérôme, whose realistic academic style of art complemented
the Orientalist subject matter, fed the public's passion for
the exotic through his paintings, prints, and sculpture.

JEWEL CABINET

FRENCH, 1562, WOOD, LIMOGES ENAMELED PLAQUES.
CABINET—H: 25 ½"; W: 28"; D: 14 ¾"
CERES PLAQUE—H: 2"; W: 1 ½"

Ceres, the goddess of agriculture, is one of the mythological figures depicted by artist Jean de Court on this opulent jewel cabinet. The goddess's shimmering cobalt blue garment emphasizes the pale luminescence of her face. The artist, famous for creating gem-like tones in his enamel work, signed and dated several of the plaques. Among those represented in enamel are Achilles, Apollo, Hercules, Deianira, Nessus, Venus, Adonis, and Cupid. The cabinet, designed to resemble an architectural structure, is decorated in Venetian style, with swirling gold lines painted on a black background. This surface treatment lends a gleam to the wood that echoes the shine and sparkle of the enamels, which were produced by heat-fusing a ground glass-like substance onto metal supports.

HANAP

JOHANN ANDREAS THELOT (SILVER),
AUGSBURG, GERMANY, CIRCA 1680, IVORY, SILVER.
H: 18"; W: 11"; D: 6"

Entwined atop a silver cover chased with cherub heads and
billowing clouds, sky deities Jupiter and Juno represent the
celestial elements in this elaborate depiction of the natural
world. The terrestrial sphere, represented by a violent
hunting scene, encompasses the shell-shaped body of the
goblet. Neptune, god of the sea, and Amphitrite his wife,
hold up the boat-like earth while standing amidst a seething
morass of fish and sea monsters attacking each other. The
fine, even texture of ivory as a carving medium enables
artists to achieve an intricacy of detail possible in few other
materials; it has allowed Jupiter's world-weary expression to
be perfectly captured in miniature.

FIREBACK

ORIGIN NOT KNOWN, DATE NOT KNOWN, IRON.

H: 82"; W: 91"

Engineered to protect the back of the hearth and to reflect a fire's warmth into the room, firebacks—large metal plates—were also embellished to serve a decorative function. The partial inscription— "CHATEAU...JOURS"—at the base of this imposing fireback introduces the possibility that the iron panel was once part of the French mantel installed in Casa Grande's Assembly Room. However, detailed shipping records of the mantel's parts do not substantiate this speculation. The cause of the roughly circular gap and lengthy split in the metal is also shrouded in mystery, and has been attributed to the impact of a cannon ball. Whatever its beginnings, the sinister face dominating the center of the fireback would have appeared even more demonic behind the roaring flames of a crackling fire.

HERALDIC BANNER

SPANISH, 17TH CENTURY, VELVET, EMBROIDERY.

H: 64"; W: 53"

From ancient to modern times, throughout the world, lions have been respected and admired for their physical beauty as well as for their strength, courage, and majesty. Two lions— symbols of royalty—support a shield that bears the arms of Spain, encircled by flags that represent various cities and principalities. This stylized feline face, complemented by a curling mane embroidered in gold metallic thread, turns to stare into the distance, on guard. The banner, one of a pair purchased at auction in 1920, hangs over a staircase in Casa del Mar, the largest of the estate's three guesthouses.

PHOTOGRAPH OF
WILLIAM RANDOLPH HEARST

CIRCA 1934.

H: 8"; W: 10"

William Randolph Hearst made his first trip to Europe
when he was ten years old. This year-and-a-half-long grand
tour with his mother, Phoebe Apperson Hearst, instilled
in him a passion for art, history, architecture, and travel.
As an adult he returned to the Continent frequently, and
in later years hosted groups of friends and family, sharing
with them his vast knowledge of the sites they visited. This
candid travel photo of Hearst suggests his background as a
newspaperman with a camera in his hand and a speculative
look on his face.

BOTTLE

CHINESE, LATE 18TH–EARLY 19TH CENTURY, PORCELAIN.
H: 12 ¼"; DIAMETER: 6"

Lotus flowers, peaches, and pomegranates fill a verdant
garden where a grinning child joins his laughing friends.
The Ch'ing period bottle displays the type of opaque enamel
decoration called famille rose, named for the predominant
rose pink shade. A lively, colorful counterpart to the somber
stone mantel upon which it rests, this delicate porcelain
piece demonstrates a single facet of the international nature
of the ceramics at San Simeon. A broad range of cultures
is represented in the collection: ancient Greek, Etruscan,
Islamic, Italian, English, and French.

"DIANA AND THE STAG"

AFTER THE ANTIQUE, CARLO FRETER, ITALIAN,

CIRCA 1930, MARBLE.

H: 82"; W: 52"; D: 42"

San Simeon's atmospheric indoor Roman Pool, meant
to emulate the splendor of Byzantium, shares space with
modern sculptures modeled on classic precedents. Diana,
both huntress and guardian of wild beasts, is depicted
midstride. She reaches for an arrow with one hand while the
other rests on an unidentifiable piece of marble that is the
sole remnant of her bow in the original ancient sculpture—
called variously, "Diane Chasseresse," "Diana of Ephesus,"
"Diane à la Biche," or "Diane de Versailles"—now in the
Louvre. The chiseled lines of the leaping deer's pale profile
stand in sharp contrast to the backdrop of multi-hued glass
mosaic tiles that depict energetic marine motifs.

DOOR GRILLE

ED TRINKKELLER, AMERICAN, 1924, WROUGHT IRON,
GOLD PAINT.

H: 85"; W: 47"; D: 1"

Architect Julia Morgan perpetuated the Arts and Crafts
tradition of utilizing highly skilled craftsmen to create
decorative and functional architectural elements in the
buildings she designed. Miss Morgan first collaborated
with metalworker Ed Trinkkeller on the 1915 construction
of Hearst's Los Angeles Examiner Building, and was so
impressed with the result that she engaged his services
for projects at San Simeon. One example of Trinkkeller's
work is the wrought-iron door grille at the courtyard
entrance of Casa del Sol guesthouse, which features the
caricatures that were his specialty. The inclusion of a self-
portrait reveals both his sense of humor and his talent for
capturing likenesses.

TABLE LAMP

CHINESE, 19TH-CENTURY CARVING, TURQUOISE, WOOD.
LAMP—H: 21"; W: 16"; D: 10"
TURQUOISE CARVING—H: 4 ¾"; W: 4"; D: 2 ½"

Wearing cheerful expressions, two female figures wield
ceremonial items—one a fan, the other a fly whisk—in the
carving on this lamp located in Casa del Monte guesthouse.
One approach to household decoration is to transform art
from the past into objects with a new use. Adapting Chinese
stone carvings into lighting fixtures was a popular practice
in the 1930s, and the turquoise sculpture had already
been made into a lamp when it was purchased by Hearst
at auction in 1931. Many of Hearst Castle's bedrooms are
illuminated by lamps carved of carnelian, jade, rose quartz,
and rock crystal.

MARRIAGE CHEST

SPANISH, 16TH CENTURY, WOOD, GILT, POLYCHROME.
H: 27"; W: 50"; D: 22 ¼"

Hidden on the underside of the chest's lid, this sumptuously
painted panel illustrates an apocryphal scene from *The
Golden Legend* of Jacobus de Voragine. Years after Christ's
crucifixion, resurrection, and ascension, the apostle Peter,
fleeing persecution in the city of Rome, unexpectedly
encounters Christ bearing His cross. Stunned, Peter asks,
"Domine quo vadis?" meaning "Master, where are you
going?" Christ replies, "To Rome, to be crucified anew."
Ashamed of his cowardice, Peter returns to Rome to endure
eventual martyrdom. In artistic tradition, Saint Peter often
appears as an older man with a square jaw framed by a short
curly gray beard.

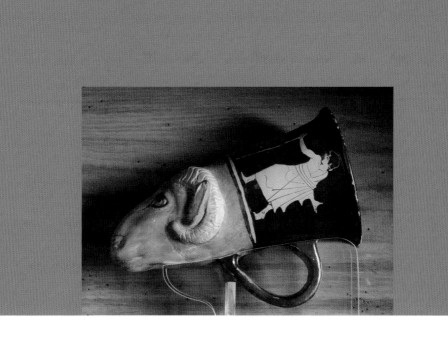

RHYTON

ATTIC RED-FIGURE, PAINTER OF BOLOGNA,

CIRCA 450–400 B.C., TERRA-COTTA, BLACK GLAZE,

RED AND WHITE SLIP.

H: 4 ¼"; W: 4 ¼"; D: 7 ¾"

A rhyton is an ancient Greek drinking horn in the shape of an animal or human head. The sculpted ram, with elaborately painted eyes and modeled horns, serves as the base of the cup, which would make it impossible to set down until empty. Painted figures of a woman and two youths stride purposefully around the mouth of the cup. This rhyton is one of several in William Randolph Hearst's collection, which includes two bulls, a griffin, a boar, and a horse. Following a time-honored tradition practiced in many of history's great houses, Hearst displayed his collection of Greek ceramics in the library of his residence. Most of the 155 pieces (including five Etruscan examples) remaining at San Simeon are still displayed in the same way.

STATUE

ITALIAN IN ANCIENT ROMAN STYLE,
PROBABLY 17TH CENTURY, LIMESTONE.
H: APPROXIMATELY 96"

Beard blowing in a breeze off the nearby Pacific, Neptune,
god of the sea, holds court over another body of water,
Hearst's lavish Neptune Pool, one of the most recognized
features of the estate. The temple, where he is the
central figure of the pediment, is a composite of ancient
architectural elements and more recent sculpture, assembled
with modern materials. It was modeled on the Temple of
Aesculapius at the Villa Borghese in Rome.

TILE

AMERICAN, 20TH CENTURY, GLAZED TERRA-COTTA.
H: 6 ¾"; W: 14 ¾"

Generous use of cool, colorful tiles, indoors and out, links
the San Simeon estate to the Mediterranean and Islamic
worlds that inspired William Randolph Hearst and Julia
Morgan. Here, a mermaid admiring her reflection in a
handheld mirror is captured in the design of a floor tile
located in Hearst's bedroom in Casa del Mar. Named for its
view of the Pacific Ocean, this guesthouse follows an aquatic
scheme of decoration that includes seahorses, mer-goats,
and fanciful dolphins. The mermaid tile was most likely
fabricated by manufacturers California Faience or Solon
and Schemmel from drawings by Julia Morgan. Produced
by the *cuenca* technique, in which flat areas of color are
separated by thin, raised lines of clay, it typifies a marriage of
traditional processes and modern forms.

WINE COOLER

DAVID WILLAUME, LONDON, 1710, SILVER.

H: 17 ¾"; W: 31"; D: 18"

David Willaume (1678–1741), a Huguenot refugee silversmith in London, created this imposing wine cooler which was used to chill bottles of wine by packing them in ice. Willaume imported the French tradition of craftsmanship that emphasized heavy cast work and applied decoration, a technique that required the use of large amounts of silver. The chunky griffin heads on opposite ends of the wine cooler reflect this working method. Although the entire body of this creature is not visible, the feline ears and fur, combined with the eagle's curved beak identify this mythological beast. An important part the silver collection, the wine cooler is prominently displayed in Casa Grande's dining hall, the Refectory, as it was in Hearst's era.

CASSONE PANEL

ITALIAN, 15TH CENTURY, OIL ON WOOD.
H: 20½"; W: 78"

The "Justice of Trajan" from Dante Alighieri's *The Divine Comedy* tells the story of a widow who confronts Roman emperor Trajan as he departs for war. She demands justice for the killing of her son by Trajan's who, while racing his horse through the city streets, trampled the widow's son to death. In one of three known versions of the story, Trajan gives his son to the widow to be her adoptive child, as evidenced in the right-hand scene of the cassone panel in Hearst's collection. The artist highlighted Trajan's concerned face by placing it against a stark white background. The cassone panel is originally from the front of one of a pair of marriage chests commissioned for the wedding between Polissena d'Este and Giovanni Romei in Ferrara in 1468.

"CIRCE"

EDITH WOODMAN BURROUGHS (1871–1916), AMERICAN,
1907, BRONZE.
H: 20 ½"; W: 8"; D: 7"

The powerful enchantress, Circe, lived on the isle of Aeaea.
Odysseus (or Ulysses), whose seafaring adventures are
chronicled in Homer's *Odyssey*, sent a group of his men
to her palace seeking hospitality. She entertained them
lavishly, but then turned them into swine; although animal
in form, they retained their human intellect. Burroughs's
sculpture captures the arrogant Circe's satisfied expression
and contorted pose as she snaps her fingers, the transformed
sailors now pigs at her feet. Signed and dated by the artist,
this bronze is a version of the original, for which Burroughs
won the Shaw Memorial Prize at the National Academy in
New York in 1907.

"MINERVA"

EMMANUEL FREMIET (1824–1910), FRENCH,
19TH CENTURY, GILT BRONZE.
H: 38"; W: 20"; D: 32 ½"

Minerva, also known as Pallas Athena, began life in an
extraordinary fashion. Fully grown, armor-clad, and
motherless, this goddess emerged from the head of her
father Zeus. Recognized for her war-like characteristics,
she appears here in battle chariot replete with three spirited
war horses. With a firm hand on the reins, Minerva uses
her invention—the bridle—to guide her steeds. The central
stallion, prancing and triumphant from battle, appears to
trumpet their victory.

"SIRÈNES"

LALIQUE, FRENCH, EARLY 20TH CENTURY, FROSTED GLASS.
H: 14"; W: 9 ½"; D: 4"

Kneeling like a classical goddess on the stopper for this
decorative bottle, René Lalique's siren arranges a garland of
flowers in her hair. Her demure countenance contradicts her
unreserved pose. This bottle is a good example of the Lalique
style that spanned the traditions of both Art Nouveau and
Art Deco. Art Nouveau celebrated the flowing motifs found
in nature while Art Deco featured crisp lines and geometric
shapes, often combined with sinuous figures. Lalique
originally made jewelry and one-of-a-kind art glass pieces,
but later mass-manufactured a variety of glass objects, like
this bottle, featured in his company's 1932 catalogue.

PERSIAN CARPET

TABRIZ/MESHED, CIRCA 1930, WOOL.
H: 78"; W: 55"

Its tranquil pose—afloat on an azure pond—belies this
duck's wide-eyed look of horror that reflects the scene taking
place above it: in the tree, an enormous serpent, jaws agape,
prepares to devour a nest of baby birds. Hand-knotted
Persian carpets of infinite variety decorate most of the rooms
at Hearst Castle. Rugs featuring complex geometric and
floral patterns or even narrative scenes, such as this one,
are used on the floors of some of the rooms, while they
ornament the walls of others.

STATUE

EGYPTIAN, 18TH DYNASTY (1580–1350 B.C.),
BLACK GRANITE.
H: 23"; W: 10"; D: 14½"

Sekhmet, a war-like goddess with the body of a woman and
the head of a lion, here wears on her head the solar disk and
uraeus (or sacred asp, denoting supreme power). Animals
were closely connected to worship in Egyptian culture,
and many gods were represented as animal-headed figures.
Architect Julia Morgan combined four Sekhmet sculptures
to create a dramatic fountain grouping on Hearst Castle's
Esplanade. Specially designed Egyptian-themed tiles and
stonework showcase the ancient representations of the
leonine protectress and avenger.

POLYCHROME STATUE

SPANISH, 17TH CENTURY, WOOD, GILT,
POLYCHROME, GLASS.
H: 33"; W: 17 ¼"; D: 12"

A contemplative young Virgin Mary holds a book in which
she has written her prayer of praise, found in the New
Testament (Luke 1: 46–55), and traditionally known as the
Magnificat. Mary's large downcast eyes, crafted from glass,
help create a life-like presence. She is dressed in a type of
garment with a laced bodice and split sleeves and skirt
that was fashionable in Spain in the last half of the 17th
century. Enhancing the illusion of realism is the girl's gown,
decorated to produce the appearance of rich fabric using
a technique called *"estofado."* The carved wood was gilded,
then painted over, and a pattern was scratched through the
paint to reveal the gold beneath.

TABLE

ITALIAN, 16TH CENTURY, WALNUT.
H: 35 ½"; W: 149"; D: 50 ½"

Originally constructed to be dismantled for relative ease
of movement, this walnut table is made of four pieces held
together by gravity and thick wooden pegs. The imposing
bulk of the tabletop overshadows the anthropomorphic
sun faces carved in low relief, one on each support. Such a
massive piece of furniture is easily accommodated by the size
of William Randolph Hearst's private Gothic Study, which
was not part of Casa Grande's original design. Extensive
demolition and reconstruction resulted in a light-filled space
Julia Morgan described as scrumptious.

PORTRAIT BUST

FERDINANDO II DE'MEDICI, GRAND DUKE OF TUSCANY,

ITALIAN (FLORENTINE), 17TH CENTURY,

MARBLE ON WOOD BASE.

H: 26"; W: 21"; D: 11"

Comparison with other portraits of both Philip II of Spain
(ruled 1556–1598) and Ferdinando II de'Medici (ruled 1621–
1670), reveals that the true identity of the sitter with the
dashing moustache was the Grand Duke of Tuscany, rather
than the King of Spain, as is mistakenly inscribed on the
base. Following Florentine tradition, sculpture of the current
ruler would have been placed over exterior doors; the piece's
condition indicates that it has spent considerable time
outside, as it would have in Florence, further corroborating
its identification as an Italian sculpture of an Italian subject.

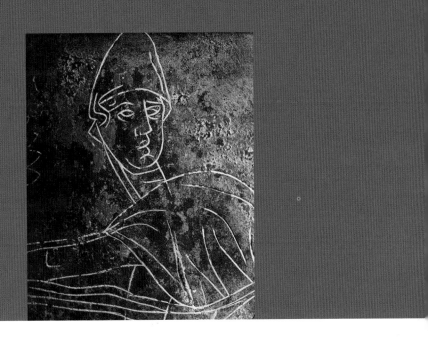

CISTA

ETRUSCAN, 3RD CENTURY B.C., BRONZE.
H: 16"; DIAMETER: 9 ½"

The lively charioteer drives his four horses around the
surface of this cylindrical receptacle while Nike, goddess of
victory, prepares to bestow the wreath that is his prize. His
face, simply delineated, eerily foreshadows the drawing style
of Pablo Picasso. Made not far from Rome, in Praeneste
(modern-day Palestrina), this cista would have been used
to hold toilet articles such as mirrors, combs, pins, and
various cosmetics.

"GALATEA ON A DOLPHIN"

LEOPOLDO ANSIGLIONI (1832–1894), ITALIAN, CIRCA 1884,

MARBLE, BRONZE.

H: 72"; W: 30"; D: 57"

In the last quarter of the 19th century, patron of the
arts Phoebe Apperson Hearst commissioned Leopoldo
Ansiglioni to carve the sea nymph Galatea. After he
completed the commission, Ansiglioni—pleading financial
hardship—persuaded Mrs. Hearst to allow him to sell the
first "Galatea," which is now at Avery Hill Winter Garden
in London. He later created a near-identical piece, which
eventually became the focal point of the quatrefoil lily pond
on the main terrace of William Randolph Hearst's California
estate. The languid nymph, surrounded by bronze sea turtles
and aquatic birds, reclines on the back of a dolphin, her
windswept hair billowing around her pensive face.

STATUE

SPANISH, 15TH CENTURY, LIMESTONE.

Covered with shaggy hair and bearing a club, a sword, and a shield, this grimacing wild man represents the sometimes uneasy mixture of untamed nature and the civilization of humankind. One of two wild men placed in architectural niches flanking the main entrance of Casa Grande, this sentinel is a deliberate tribute to a medieval example. In a 1919 letter, Hearst instructed architect Julia Morgan to incorporate design elements that featured guardian wild men, such as the ones found on a church doorway from Seville, Spain; Hearst even provided Morgan with a photograph of the doorway, published in a book about the architecture of southern Spain.

CARYATID

VAN DER LOO FAMILY, AMERICAN, 1930,

CAST STONE, GILT, POLYCHROME.

H: APPROXIMATELY 180"; W: 59"; D: 24"

Gazing out over Hearst's private theater, this caryatid—a
column or support sculpted in the shape of a female
figure—is one of fourteen stylized beauties holding
bouquets of electric lights. Because of his involvement
in the film industry, Hearst and his companion, actress
Marion Davies, often entertained Hollywood notables;
the screening of after-dinner movies was a tradition at San
Simeon. Although this home theater is less opulent than the
commercial movie palaces that were common to the era, the
lush seats, sumptuous red silk wall hangings, and imposing
caryatids combined to provide a memorable experience for
Hearst's guests.

MOSAIC

ROMAN, 2ND–3RD CENTURY, MARBLE.
H: 131"; W: 156"

The fearsome fish bares a row of sharp teeth as he glides
across the white marble pavement he shares with another
fish, a merman, and an octopus. Currently located in the
vestibule of Casa Grande, the mosaic floor, replete with
black-and-white marine motifs, likely originated near Rome
in Ostia, a shipping center at the mouth of the Tiber River.
During conservation treatment, scientific analysis of the
tesserae—the small tiles that compose the pattern—revealed
the pieces to be from not only Italy, but also Egypt and
Greece, a testimony in stone to the Roman Empire's far-
reaching trade resources.

TAPESTRY

FLEMISH, 17TH CENTURY, WOOL, SILK.
H: 119"; W: 142"

Most world cultures have developed some type of tapestry-weaving technique. Subjects are taken from religion, myth, legend, history, war, symbolism, recreation, and daily life. In seventeenth-century Europe, woven landscapes featuring villagers at work or play satisfied the popular taste for "reality" and the familiar. This scene is one of a series of tapestries believed to depict months of the year. The figures perform agricultural tasks such as bee-keeping, tree-grafting, and berry-picking. A woman in an elegantly brocaded gown observes the laborer who employs grafting tools while her companion points to the branch in seeming explanation of the process. The clean lines of the basket-carrying maiden's profile contrast with the intricate design of her head-wrap.

COVERED JAR

SÈVRES, FRENCH, 20TH CENTURY, GLAZED PORCELAIN.
H: 14 ½"; DIAMETER: 9"

Exotic animals decorate the surface of this porcelain jar, and
a three-dimensional chimpanzee gazes quizzically from his
perch on the lid. Transparent, thick purple glaze enhances
the jar's color but gently blurs the ape's features. The Sèvres
porcelain factory was established in the 18th century under
French royal patronage, and is probably best known for its
elaborate, fragile-looking, hand-painted and gilded porcelain
pieces. This sturdy example from the 1920s reflects the
influence of Art Deco on the Sèvres style, and is signed by
designer Maurice Gensoli, who worked as a decorator at
Sèvres during the 1920s and served as the first director of the
faience department.

EYE-CUP

ATTIC BLACK-FIGURE, CIRCA 530–520 B.C.,

TERRA-COTTA, BLACK GLAZE, RED AND WHITE SLIP.

H: 5 ¼"; W: 15 ½"; D: 12 ¾"

Ancient Greeks used a variety of containers to hold a
mixture of water and wine. This type of drinking cup, or
kylix, is characterized by its wide shallow bowl balanced on
a stemmed foot. The decoration is fitting: a painted mask
of Dionysus, the god of wine. The bearded deity is crowned
with an ivy wreath, his hypnotic gaze mirrored by the
large eyes that flank him. These eyes serve to transform the
entire vessel into the semblance of a face and to confer its
name: eye-cup.

PORTRAIT BUST

SAINT URSULA (?), ORIGIN NOT KNOWN,

PROBABLY 17TH CENTURY, SILVER.

H: 26"; W: 18"; D: 10"

An inscription on the applied medallion identifies the
subject as Saint Ursula, who, according to legend, was
the leader of eleven thousand virgins martyred in the
fifth century as they returned from a pilgrimage to Rome.
Her serene countenance was created by a technique
called repoussé, in which the design is raised in relief by
hammering on the reverse side of the metal. A removable
section at the back of her head indicates that this piece may
have functioned as a reliquary. A reliquary is a container for
the preservation or display of relics—objects associated with
a Christian saint. Other reliquaries in Hearst's collection
still contain bits of bone, cloth, and beads—simple, but
powerful remnants of the past.

ANIMAL GROUP

PROBABLY ITALIAN, 15TH CENTURY, MARBLE.
H: 28"; W: 11 ¾"; D: 22"

A pair of marble animal groups flanks the massive fireplace
in the Refectory. Even with finely carved detail, the stylized
forms prevent exact identification of the animal species. This
group probably depicts an eagle or falcon—with large eyes
and sharp, down-curved beak—standing on a fox. Purchased
at auction in 1926, these animals stood watch while William
Randolph Hearst entertained political figures, business
associates, and luminaries of the film industry.

ARCHWAY

SPANISH, 13TH CENTURY, RED PYRENEES MARBLE.
H: 164", W: 208"; D: 15"

The practice of incorporating historic building components
into the architecture of William Randolph Hearst's San
Simeon estate is exemplified in the placement of this portal
that links Casa Grande's Refectory and Morning Room. The
thirteenth-century archway from the Cathedral of Urgel
in Catalonia, Spain depicts apostles Peter and Paul, the
archangel Gabriel, and unidentified evangelists and saints
around the central figure of Christ. The female figure's
expression illustrates the rudimentary carving style of this
early period, which is an interesting counterpoint to the
arch's overall complexity.

RELIEF SCULPTURE

ENGLISH, 15TH CENTURY, ALABASTER, GILT, POLYCHROME.
H: 22"; W: 13 ½"; D: 2"

The crucified Christ, held by God the Father, with the Holy
Spirit as a dove hovering above the cross, is a conventional
composition in depicting the Trinity. Although the dove
is missing from this piece, the drilled hole where it once
rested can still be seen. In the tradition of English alabaster
carving, the relief would have been one of a series of panels
placed in a wooden framework to form an altarpiece, or
it might have served as a single devotional plaque. This
example typifies English alabaster carvers' portrayals of God
the Father: crowned, wide-eyed, and with flowing locks
and beard.

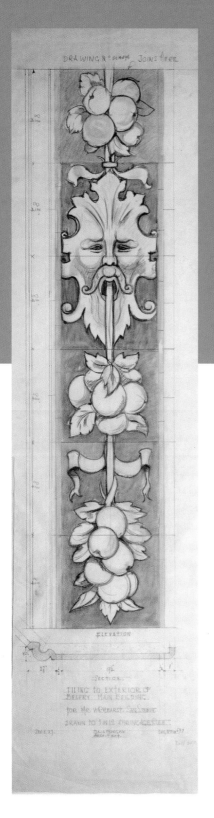

DRAWING

OFFICE OF JULIA MORGAN, AMERICAN, 1927,
CHARCOAL ON PAPER.
H: 80 ¼"; W: 24 ¾"

The green man dates back to prehistoric times.
A human face, hidden within leaves or actually
composed of them, serves as an archetype of
fertility, renewal, and rebirth. Adaptability of
the design lends itself to a variety of uses, most
notably in architecture. The theme of rebirth made
the green man particularly suitable to represent
Christian precepts of spiritual resurrection and
it was incorporated into the decoration of many
churches, especially medieval ones. This full-scale
green man drawing was created as a pattern for the
tile used on the bell towers of Casa Grande.

"PORTRAIT OF A WOMAN"

(CALLED ISABELLA D'ESTE), GUILIO CAMPI, ITALIAN, 16TH CENTURY,
OIL ON CANVAS.
H: 36 ⅝"; W: 29 ½"

While purchased by William Randolph Hearst as a portrait of
Isabella d'Este—political maven and patron of the arts in Renaissance
Italy—visual clues in this large painting conspire to cast doubt on the
identity of the subject. Described by biographers as having brown
eyes and a penchant for bleaching her hair blonde, the green-eyed
brunette staring intently from the portrait seems an unlikely match.
Historically, the nature of portraiture has frequently hindered later
attempts at positive identification of subjects, since portraits have
always depended upon prevailing artistic fashion. They are created
using the preferred styles, techniques, and media of the moment,
with an unintentional result: a sitter of sometimes uncertain identity.

TABLE LAMP

GERDAGO, 1930S, BRONZE, ENAMEL, IVORY.
H: 13"; W: 6 ¾"; D: 5 ¾"

The materials—bronze and ivory—that make up the
sculpture incorporated into this lamp have been used by
artists for centuries. However, the Art Deco style that
defines the piece was a complete departure from the
realistic-looking art of Europe's past. The harlequin figure
was created by Gerdago in the 1930s, and demonstrates a
fascination with the modern in decorative arts. Theatrical
poses and the colorfully bold patterns of futuristic costume
were part of the sculptor's trademark style. Here the
harlequin's delicately modeled carved-ivory face is in striking
contrast to the flamboyant bronze surrounding it.

PORTRAIT OF
WILLIAM RANDOLPH HEARST

ORRIN PECK, AMERICAN, 1894, OIL ON CANVAS.
H: 45 ½"; W: 40 ½"

Painted in 1894, this portrait shows William Randolph
Hearst at age thirty-one. The artist, Hearst's childhood
friend Orrin Peck, perfectly captured Hearst's predominant
facial feature: his piercing blue eyes. The portrait hangs in
the Gothic Study as it did during Mr. Hearst's day, when the
elaborate room served as the headquarters for America's first
media empire. Over half a century after this portrait was
painted, William Randolph Hearst died at the age of eighty-
eight in Beverly Hills, California, construction on his San
Simeon estate unfinished.

SOURCES

INTRODUCTION, p. 7   Charles A. Nelson, "The Development and Neural Bases of Face Recognition," *Infant and Child Development* 10 (2001): 3-18. Richard Brilliant, *Portraiture*, London, 1991, 1997, p. 9. Vicki Bruce and Andy Young, *In the Eye of the Beholder: The Science of Face Perception*, New York, 1998, pp. 4, 136. Arthur and Mildred Stapley Byne, *Decorated Wooden Ceilings in Spain: A Collection of Photographs and Measured Drawings with Descriptive Text*, New York, London, 1920, p. 22.

"BONAPARTE BEFORE THE SPHINX," p. 11   Brian M. Fagan, *The Rape of the Nile: Tomb Robbers, Tourists, & Archaeologists in Egypt*, New York, 1975, pp. 66-68. Jennifer Hardin, "From Antiquity to Exotica: Egypt and the European Artistic Experience," *The Lure of Egypt: Land of the Pharaohs Revisited*, exhibition catalogue, Museum of Fine Arts, St. Petersburg, Florida, 1996, pp. 4-9. Gerald M. Ackerman, *The Life and Work of Jean-Léon Gérôme, with a Catalogue Raisonné*, London, 1986, p. 46. Florence Rionnet, "Goupil and Gérôme: Two Views of the Sculpture Industry," *Gérôme & Goupil, Art and Enterprise*, exhibition catalogue, Musée Goupil, Paris, 2000, pp. 44-53.

JEWEL CABINET, p. 13   Susan L. Caroselli, *The Painted Enamels of Limoges: A Catalogue of the Collection of the Los Angeles County Museum of Art*, Los Angeles, 1993, p. 157. Hans Huth, *Lacquer of the West: The History of a Craft and an Industry, 1550-1950*, Chicago, 1971, pp. 6-7.

HANAP, p. 15   Jane Bassett and Peggy Fogelman, *Looking at European Sculpture: A Guide to Technical Terms*, Los Angeles, 1997, p. 49.

FIREBACK, p. 17   Alison Kelly, *The Book of English Fireplaces*, Feltham, Middlesex, England, 1968, p. 25. Elizabeth Wilhide, *The Fireplace: A Guide to Period Style*, Boston, 1994, p. 28.

HERALDIC BANNER, p. 19   Kenneth Clark, *Animals and Men: Their Relationship as Reflected in Western Art from Prehistory to the Present Day*, New York, 1977, p. 85.

PHOTOGRAPH OF WILLIAM RANDOLPH HEARST, p. 21   David Nasaw, *The Chief: The Life of William Randolph Hearst*, New York, 2000, pp. 399-404.

BOTTLE, p. 23   Michael Sullivan, *The Arts of China*, rev. ed., Berkeley and Los Angeles, 1979, pp. 248-49.

"DIANA AND THE STAG," p. 25   Charles Mills Gayley, *The Classic Myths in English Literature and in Art*, rev. ed., Boston, 1911, p. 30. Maxime Collignon, *Manual of Mythology in Relation to Greek Art*, translated and enlarged by Jane E. Harrison, London, 1890, p. 94. Francis Haskell and Nicholas Penny, *Taste and the Antique: The Lure of Classical Sculpture 1500-1900*, New Haven, 1981, p. 196.

DOOR GRILLE, p. 27   Sara Holmes Boutelle, *Julia Morgan, Architect*, New York, 1988, pp. 9, 12, 174.

TABLE LAMP, p. 29   Martin Battersby, *The Decorative Thirties*, rev. ed., Whitney Library of Design, New York, 1988, p. 123. American Art Association, Anderson Galleries, *Sale Number 3917: XVII & XVIII Century English Furniture, Silver, Tapestries, Rugs, Oriental and Other Objets d'Art*, sale catalogue, New York, October 20-24, 1931, p. 17, no. 505.

MARRIAGE CHEST, p. 31   Sally Fisher, *The Square Halo and Other Mysteries of Western Art*, New York, 1995, p. 117.

RHYTON, p. 33   J. D. Beazley, *Attic Red-figure Vase-Painters*, 2nd ed., Oxford, 1963, p. 917, no. 196. Herbert Hoffmann, *Attic Red-figured Rhyta*, Mainz, 1962, p. 33, no. 79. Vinnie Nørskov, *Greek Vases in New Contexts*, Aarhus, Denmark, 2002, p. 74.

STATUE, p. 35   Edith Wharton, *Italian Villas and Their Gardens*, Illustrated with Pictures by Maxfield Parrish, New York, 1904, p. 96.

TILE, p. 37   Tony Herbert and Kathryn Huggins, *The Decorative Tile in Architecture and Interiors*, London, 1995, p. 7. Robert C. Pavlik, "The Tile Art of San Simeon: A Social and Cultural Perspective," *Tile Heritage*, Vol. IV, No. 2 (Winter 1997/98), 2-11. Norman Karlson, *American Art Tile: 1876-1941*, New York, 1998, pp. 140-42. Noël Riley, *A History of Decorative Tiles*, Edison, NJ, 1987, reprint 1997, p. 46.

WINE COOLER, p. 39   John Fleming and Hugh Honour, *Dictionary of the Decorative Arts*, London, 1977, p. 859. J. F. Hayward, *Huguenot Silver in England 1688-1727*, London, 1959. N. M. Penzer, "The Great Wine-Coolers—I," *Apollo*, August 1957, 3-7. Hugh Tait, "Huguenot Silver Made in London (c. 1690-1723): The Peter Wilding Bequest to the British Museum, Part 1," *Connoisseur*, August 1972, 267-77.

CASSONE PANEL, p. 41   Salvatore Settis, "Traiano a Hearst Castle: Due Cassoni Estensi," *Estratto da I Tatti Studies: Essays in the Renaissance*, Vol. 6, 1995, 31-82.

"CIRCE," p. 43   Charlotte Streifer Rubinstein, *American Women Artists from Early Indian Times to the Present*, New York, 1982, p. 212.

"SIRÈNES," p. 47   Tony L. Mortimer, *Lalique*, Secaucus, NJ, 1989. (First published in London, 1989), p. 18. *Catalogue des Verreries de René Lalique*, Paris, 1932, p. 19, no. 883.

STATUE, p. 51   Richard H. Wilkinson, *The Complete Gods and Goddesses of Ancient Egypt*, London, 2003, pp. 181-82. Margaret Ellen Mayo, *Ancient Art*, Richmond, VA, 1998, pp. 14-15.

POLYCHROME STATUE, p. 53   Suzanne L. Stratton, *Spanish Polychrome Sculpture 1500-1800 in United States Collections,* exhibition catalogue, Spanish Institute, New York, Los Angeles County Museum of Art, Los Angeles, 1993, p. 143.

TABLE, p. 55   Geoffrey Beard and Victor Chinnery, "The Renaissance," in *Sotheby's Concise Encyclopedia of Furniture,* Christopher Payne, editor, London, 1989, 1994, p. 24. The Julia Morgan Collection. Special Collections, Robert E. Kennedy Library, California Polytechnic State University, San Luis Obispo, California, Julia Morgan correspondence to William Randolph Hearst, 9 October 1928.

PORTRAIT BUST, p. 57   Karla Langedijk, *The Portraits of the Medici 15th-18th Centuries, Vol. II,* Florence, 1983, p. 797, no. 63. Alan P. Darr, "The Medici and the Legacy of Michelangelo in Late Renaissance Florence: An Introduction," in *The Medici, Michelangelo, and the Art of Late Renaissance Florence,* New Haven, 2002, p. 3.

CISTA, p. 59   Mario A. Del Chiaro, "A Praenestine (Etruscan) Cista at San Simeon," *California Studies in Classical Antiquity,* Vol. 5, 1972, 95-101.

"GALATEA ON A DOLPHIN," p. 61   Bancroft Library, University of California, Berkeley, Phoebe A. Hearst Papers 72/204/C, Leopoldo Ansiglioni correspondence to Phoebe Apperson Hearst, 7 March 1882. James C. Kennedy, *Avery Hill Winter Garden,* London, 1975. Bancroft Library, University of California, Berkeley, Phoebe A. Hearst Papers 72/204/ C, Leopoldo Ansiglioni correspondence to Phoebe Apperson Hearst, 30 August 1884 [?].

STATUE, p. 63   Richard Bernheimer, *Wild Men in the Middle Ages: A Study in Art, Sentiment and Demonology,* New York, 1970, pp. 1-5. The Julia Morgan Collection. Special Collections, Robert E. Kennedy Library, California Polytechnic State University, San Luis Obispo, California, William Randolph Hearst correspondence to Julia Morgan, 10 December 1919. Austin Whittlesey, *The Minor Ecclesiastical, Domestic and Garden Architecture of Southern Spain,* 2nd ed., New York, 1917, p. 48.

CARYATID, p. 65   W. A. Swanberg, *Citizen Hearst,* New York, 1961, reprint 1986, p. 542. Sara Holmes Boutelle, *Julia Morgan, Architect,* New York, 1988, pp. 196-97.

MOSAIC, p. 67   Peter Fischer, *Mosaic: History and Technique,* London, 1971, p. 54. Caroline Suter and Celia Gregory, *The Art of Mosaic,* London, 2001, p. 10. Stanley V. Margolis, "Analysis of Marble Tiles from Roman Floor Mosaic from Hearst Castle, San Simeon, California, May 15, 1987," pp. 4-6, in *The Conservation and Restoration of the Roman Marble Mosaic Pavement PC 5755 Hearst San Simeon State Historical Monument,* Zdravko Barov and Constance Faber, conservation report, San Simeon, California, 1988.

TAPESTRY, p. 69   Barty Phillips, *Tapestry,* London, 1994, p. 16. Anna Gray Bennett, *Five Centuries of Tapestry from The Fine Arts Museums of San Francisco,* rev. ed., San Francisco, 1992, p. 163.

COVERED JAR, p. 71   Jerry E. Patterson, *Porcelain,* The Smithsonian Illustrated Library of Antiques, Washington, D. C., 1979, pp. 67-68. Arie Van De Lemme, *A Guide to Art Deco Style,* London, 1986, reprint 1997, p. 87. Victor Arwas, *Art Deco,* rev. ed., New York, 1992, pp. 278-79.

EYE-CUP, p. 73   Joseph Veach Noble, *The Techniques of Painted Attic Pottery,* New York, 1965, pp. 20-21. J. D. Beazley, *Attic Black-figure Vase-painters,* Oxford, 1956, reprint edition, New York, 1978, pp. 205-207. Evelyn Elizabeth Bell, "Two Krokotos Mask Cups at San Simeon," *California Studies in Classical Antiquity,* Vol. 10, 1977, 266-92.

ARCHWAY, p. 79   Joan-Albert Adell et al, *La Catedral de la Seu d'Urgell,* Manresa and Barcelona, 2000, pp. 161-63.

RELIEF SCULPTURE, p. 81   Sally Fisher, *The Square Halo and Other Mysteries of Western Art,* New York, 1995, pp. 84-85. Francis Cheetham, *Alabaster Images of Medieval England,* Woodbridge, Suffolk, England, 2003, pp. 150-51. Francis Cheetham, *English Medieval Alabasters: With a Catalogue of the Collection in the Victoria and Albert Museum,* new ed., Woodbridge, Suffolk, England, 2005, p. 28.

DRAWING, p. 83   Ronald Sheridan and Anne Ross, *Gargoyles and Grotesques: Paganism in the Medieval Church,* Boston, 1975, pp. 31-32. Kathleen Basford, *The Green Man,* Suffolk, England and Rochester, New York, 1978, reprint 2003, p. 7.

"PORTRAIT OF A WOMAN," p. 85   Burton B. Fredericksen, *Handbook of the Paintings in the Hearst San Simeon State Historical Monument,* n.p., 1976, no. 39. Edith Patterson Meyer, *First Lady of the Renaissance: A Biography of Isabella d'Este,* Boston, 1970, p. 8. George R. Marek, *The Bed and the Throne: The Life of Isabella d'Este,* New York, 1976, pp. 33-34. Shearer West, *Portraiture,* Oxford History of Art, Oxford, 2004, p. 11. Richard Brilliant, *Portraiture,* London, 1991, reprint 1997, p. 62.

TABLE LAMP, p. 87   Nicholas Penny, *The Materials of Sculpture,* New Haven, CT, 1993, pp. 153, 219. Victor Arwas, *Art Deco,* New York, 1980, pp. 17, 162.

PORTRAIT OF WILLIAM RANDOLPH HEARST, p. 89   David Nasaw, *The Chief: The Life of William Randolph Hearst,* New York, 2000, pp. 443-44.

BIBLIOGRAPHY

Ackerman, Gerald M. *The Life and Work of Jean-Léon Gérôme, with a Catalogue Raisonné.* London: Sotheby's Publications, 1986.

Adell, Joan-Albert, et al. *La Catedral de la Seu d'Urgell.* Manresa and Barcelona: Angle Editorial, 2000.

American Art Association, Anderson Galleries. *Sale Number 3917: XVII & XVIII Century English Furniture, Silver, Tapestries, Rugs, Oriental and Other Objects d'Art.* New York: Anderson Galleries, October 20-24, 1931.

Arwas, Victor. *Art Deco.* New York: Abrams, 1980.

———. *Art Deco,* rev. ed. New York: Abrams, 1992.

Bancroft Library, University of California, Berkeley, Phoebe A. Hearst Papers. 72/204/C.

Basford, Kathleen. *The Green Man.* Suffolk, England and Rochester, NY: D. S. Brewer/Boydell & Brewer, 1978, reprint, 2003.

Bassett, Jane, and Peggy Fogelman. *Looking at European Sculpture: A Guide to Technical Terms.* Los Angeles: Getty Publications, 1997.

Battersby, Martin. *The Decorative Thirties,* rev. ed. Whitney Library of Design. New York: Watson-Guptill, 1988. First published 1971.

Beazley, J. D. *Attic Black-figure Vase-Painters.* Oxford: Clarendon Press, 1956. Reprint, New York: Hacker Art Books, 1978.

———. *Attic Red-figure Vase-Painters,* 2nd ed. Oxford: Oxford University Press, 1963.

Bell, Evelyn Elizabeth. "Two Krokotos Mask Cups at San Simeon." *California Studies in Classical Antiquity,* 10 (1977): 266-92.

Bennett, Anna Gray. *Five Centuries of Tapestry from The Fine Arts Museums of San Francisco,* rev. ed. San Francisco: The Fine Arts Museums of San Francisco and Chronicle Books, 1992.

Bernheimer, Richard. *Wild Men in the Middle Ages: A Study in Art,*

Sentiment and Demonology. New York: Octagon Books, 1970.

Boutelle, Sara Holmes. *Julia Morgan, Architect.* New York: Abbeville, 1988.

Brilliant, Richard. *Portraiture.* London: Reaktion Books, 1991, reprint 1997.

Bruce, Vicki, and Andy Young. *In the Eye of the Beholder: The Science of Face Perception.* New York: Oxford University Press, 1998.

Byne, Arthur, and Mildred Stapley Byne. *Decorated Wooden Ceilings in Spain: A Collection of Photographs and Measured Drawings with Descriptive Text.* New York: G. P. Putnam's Sons, 1920.

Caroselli, Susan L. *The Painted Enamels of Limoges: A Catalogue of the Collection of the Los Angeles County Museum of Art.* Los Angeles: Los Angeles County Museum of Art, 1993.

Catalogue des Verreries de René Lalique. Paris: Lalique & Cie, 1932.

Cheetham, Francis. *Alabaster Images of Medieval England.* Woodbridge, Suffolk, England: The Association for Cultural Exchange and The Boydell Press, 2003.

———. *English Medieval Alabasters: With a Catalogue of the Collection in the Victoria and Albert Museum,* New Edition. Woodbridge, Suffolk, England: The Association for Cultural Exchange and The Boydell Press, 2005. First published 1984 by Phaidon.

Clark, Kenneth. *Animals and Men: Their Relationship as Reflected in Western Art from Prehistory to the Present Day.* New York: William Morrow, 1977.

Collignon, Maxime. *Manual of Mythology in Relation to Greek Art.* Translated and enlarged by Jane E. Harrison. London: H. Grevel, 1890.

Darr, Alan P. "The Medici and the Legacy of Michelangelo in Late Renaissance Florence: An Introduction." In *The Medici, Michelangelo, and the Art of Late Renaissance Florence.* New Haven, CT: Yale University Press

in association with the Detroit Institute of Arts, 2002.

Del Chiaro, Mario A. "A Praenestine (Etruscan) Cista at San Simeon." *California Studies in Classical Antiquity* 5 (1972): 95-101.

Fagan, Brian M. *The Rape of the Nile: Tomb Robbers, Tourists, & Archaeologists in Egypt.* New York: Charles Scribner's Sons, 1975.

Fischer, Peter. *Mosaic: History and Technique.* London: Thames & Hudson, 1971.

Fisher, Sally. *The Square Halo and Other Mysteries of Western Art.* New York: Abrams, 1995.

Fleming, John, and Hugh Honour. *Dictionary of the Decorative Arts.* London: Harper & Row, 1977.

Fredericksen, Burton B. *Handbook of the Paintings in the Hearst San Simeon State Historical Monument.* N.p.: Delphinian Publications in cooperation with The California Department of Parks and Recreation, 1976.

Fredericksen, Burton B., and Federico Zeri. *Census of Pre-Nineteenth-Century Italian Paintings in North American Public Collections.* Cambridge, MA: Harvard University Press, 1972.

Gayley, Charles Mills. *The Classic Myths in English Literature and in Art,* rev. ed. Boston: Ginn & Co., 1911. First published 1893.

Hardin, Jennifer. "From Antiquity to Exotica: Egypt and the European Artistic Experience." In *The Lure of Egypt: Land of the Pharaohs Revisited,* exhibition catalogue. St. Petersburg, FL: Museum of Fine Arts, St. Petersburg, 1996.

Haskell, Francis, and Nicholas Penny. *Taste and the Antique: The Lure of Classical Sculpture 1500-1900.* New Haven, CT: Yale University Press, 1981.

Hayward, J. F. *Huguenot Silver in England 1688-1727.* London: Faber and Faber, 1959.

Herbert, Tony, and Kathryn Huggins. *The Decorative Tile in Architecture and Interiors.* London: Phaidon, 1995.

Hoffman, Herbert. *Attic Red-figured Rhyta.* Mainz: Verlag Philipp von Zabern, 1962.

Huth, Hans. *Lacquer of the West: The History of a Craft and an Industry, 1550-1950.* Chicago: University of Chicago Press, 1971.

The Julia Morgan Collection. Special Collections, Robert E. Kennedy Library, California Polytechnic State University, San Luis Obispo, California.

Karlson, Norman. *American Art Tile: 1876-1941.* New York: Rizzoli, 1998.

Kelly, Alison. *The Book of English Fireplaces.* Feltham, Middlesex, England: Country Life Books, 1968.

Kennedy, James C. *Avery Hill Winter Garden.* London: Greater London Council, 1975.

Langedijk, Karla. *The Portraits of the Medici 15th-18th Centuries, Vol. II.* Florence: Studio per Edizioni Scelte, 1983.

Marek, George R. *The Bed and the Throne: The Life of Isabella d'Este.* New York: Harper & Row, 1976.

Margolis, Stanley V. "Analysis of Marble Tiles from Roman Floor Mosaic from Hearst Castle, San Simeon, California. May 15, 1987." In *The Conservation and Restoration of the Roman Marble Mosaic Pavement PC 5755 Hearst San Simeon State Historical Monument.* Zdravko Barov and Constance Faber. Conservation Report, Hearst Castle, 1988.

Mayo, Margaret Ellen. *Ancient Art.* Richmond, VA: Virginia Museum of Fine Arts, 1998.

Meyer, Edith Patterson. *First Lady of the Renaissance: A Biography of Isabella d'Este.* Boston: Little, Brown, 1970.

Mortimer, Tony L. *Lalique.* Secaucus, NJ: Chartwell Books, 1989. First published 1989 by Pyramid, an imprint of the Octopus Publishing Group, London.

Nasaw, David. *The Chief: The Life of William Randolph Hearst.* New York: Houghton Mifflin, 2000.

Nelson, Charles A. "The Development and Neural Bases of Face Recognition." *Infant and Child Development* 10 (2001): 3-18.

Noble, Joseph Veach. *The Techniques of Painted Attic Pottery.* New York: Watson-Guptill and The Metropolitan Museum of Art, 1965.

Nørskov, Vinnie. *Greek Vases in New Contexts.* Aarhus, Denmark: Aarhus University Press, 2002.

Patterson, Jerry E. *Porcelain.* The Smithsonian Illustrated Library of Antiques. Washington, D.C.: Cooper-Hewitt Museum/Smithsonian Institution, 1979.

Pavlik, Robert C. "The Tile Art of San Simeon: A Social and Cultural Perspective." *Tile Heritage* Vol. IV, No. 2 (Winter 1997/98): 2-11.

Penny, Nicholas. *The Materials of Sculpture.* New Haven, CT: Yale University Press, 1993.

Penzer, N. M. "The Great Wine-Coolers—I." *Apollo: The Magazine of the Arts for Collectors and Connoisseurs* (August, 1957): 3-7.

Phillips, Barty. *Tapestry.* London: Phaidon, 1994.

Riley, Noël. *A History of Decorative Tiles.* Edison, NJ: Chartwell Books, 1987, reprint 1997.

Rionnet, Florence. "Goupil and Gérôme: Two Views of the Sculpture Industry." In *Gérôme and Goupil, Art and Enterprise,* exhibition catalogue. Paris: Musée Goupil, 2000.

Rubinstein, Charlotte Streifer. *American Women Artists from Early Indian Times to the Present.* New York: Avon, 1982.

Settis, Salvatore. *Traiano a Hearst Castle: Due Cassoni Estensi.* Estratto da I Tatti Studies: Essays in the Renaissance, Vol. 6, 1995. Leo S. Olschki Editore. Florence: 1996.

Sheridan, Ronald, and Anne Ross. *Gargoyles and Grotesques: Paganism in the Medieval Church.* Boston: New York Graphic Society, 1975.

Sotheby's Concise Encyclopedia of Furniture. Christopher Payne, editor. London: Conran Octopus, 1989, reprint 1994.

Stratton, Suzanne L. *Spanish Polychrome Sculpture 1500-1800 in United States Collections,* exhibition catalogue. New York and Los Angeles: Spanish Institute and Los Angeles County Museum of Art, 1993.

Sullivan, Michael. *The Arts of China,* rev. ed. Berkeley and Los Angeles: University of California Press, reprint with corrections 1979. First published 1967.

Suter, Caroline, and Celia Gregory. *The Art of Mosaic.* London: Aquamarine/Anness Publishing, 2001.

Swanberg, W.A. *Citizen Hearst.* New York: Scribner/Collier, 1961, reprint 1986.

Tait, Hugh. "Huguenot Silver Made in London (c. 1690-1723): The Peter Wilding Bequest to the British Museum, Part 1." *Connoisseur* (1972): 267-77.

Van de Lemme, Arie. *A Guide to Art Deco Style.* London: Grange Books, 1986, reprint 1997.

West, Shearer. *Portraiture.* Oxford History of Art. Oxford: Oxford University Press, 2004.

Wharton, Edith. *Italian Villas and Their Gardens.* Illustrated with Pictures by Maxfield Parrish. New York: Century, 1904.

Whittlesey, Austin. *The Minor Ecclesiastical, Domestic and Garden Architecture of Southern Spain,* 2nd ed. New York: The Architectural Book Publishing Co., 1917.

Wilhide, Elizabeth. *The Fireplace: A Guide to Period Style.* Boston: Little, Brown, 1994.

Wilkinson, Richard H. *The Complete Gods and Goddesses of Ancient Egypt.* London: Thames & Hudson, 2003.

INDEX

HEARST CASTLE
PRESS